Yes, You Can!

Full-time RVing for the Single Person

By: Joy Ethridge

Dedication
This book is dedicated to my sister-in-law Carol Killingsworth. Without her encouragement and belief in me, I would not be living my dream.

Published by Lulu.com

ISBN 978-14303-1284-0

Table of Contents

Forward

I am asked by people all the time "how do you do it alone?" I find that even women that are fulltimers tell me they don't think they could do it alone! My answer is YES, YOU CAN!!! I am always amazed that people seem to think I am special because I RV alone. There are lots of us out there! All you have to do is believe you can and go for it!

I searched for info while I was planning my life on wheels. Everything I could find that was written for Solo Full-timers was written by people that were either married or focused on looking for that significant other. Nothing I found really went into living the RV lifestyle and making it work as a Workamper. I am not a professional writer, I make my living Workamping. I needed to hear the story from someone like me, who was out making a living as a Workamper in seasonal jobs. Don't get me wrong you will not become rich by Workamping! However you can keep bread on the table, a roof over your head and wheels under your feet.

Chapter 1
Why I began Full-timing

There are as many reasons for Full time RVing as there are people out there doing it. We all have a story to tell. The one thing we have in common is our love for the lifestyle and the freedom to roam. The thing that separates us from others is we had the faith to take the steps needed to get here, (wherever here is)! You only need a smidgen of belief in yourself to get into this new lifestyle. If I can do it so can you.

It was not my original plan to be out on the road alone. I was married for over 30 years and had planned to workamp with my husband when he retired. I thought we were married for life, he had other desires. So we parted ways. I hope he is happy with his choices. I know I have been blessed.

My life changed completely in a 6 month period of time. My first major change was of course the separation from my husband. This came about in late July. In mid September I lost hope of us being able to reunite and filed for Divorce. This in itself would have been enough

to work through, but my whole life changed. I
spent a lot of time in prayer and trying to figure
out why me! While I was at my lowest point,
going through my divorce, I had another
problem. I was in a real quandary as to what to
do with myself. I did not have a career as most
women these days do. I had been a housewife
for years and had only gone back to work six
months earlier to earn the extra money to pay
off all our bills so we would be in a good
financial position to hit the road, when my
husband retired. This is not to say I had never
worked. I had worked in retail a lot of years and
also worked several years as a Librarian.   In
just a couple of months I had worked my way
up from a part time temporary job to Operations
manager of the store where I worked. I had no
desire to move up the ladder any further and
when the manager found this out he made my
life at the store intolerable. He wanted me to
move up to the managers position so he could
move on. I was in the middle of my divorce and
the stress at work along with my personal
problems was pretty overwhelming. I had to
quit work or spend my days at work crying! So
I opted for quitting. That job represented

security for me and I probably would have stayed and continued with the everyday grind if my boss had not made it impossible for me! In looking back my life is so much better because I quit that job and moved on down the road literally!

I then took an RV trip with my brother's family. We went to Branson Missouri and Gatlinburg Tennessee. I had never been on vacation when I had so little security! No job, no husband and soon to be no home! I must say the trip was good for my soul. It was good to be with people that cared for me and the weather was great. I highly recommend taking vacations when everything else in your world has gone wrong. You come home with a new outlook and ready to face the challenges ahead.

Not long after the trip, when I was wrestling with what I was to do with myself I had a conversation with my brother and sister-in-law. She asked me what I would do if I could do anything. I told her without a moment's hesitation I would be a workamper. She said "go for it Joy. I have never known you not to be able to do anything you wanted to do". I was scared and excited all at once! Could I really follow my dream? Could I survive alone out in the RV work world? YES! This was in October and the tuning point for me. I began to look forward with positive thoughts for my future. I still have days when I think of what might have been. However I have moved forward and the future is as bright for me as it has ever been. I continue to face each day as a new opportunity.

Chapter 2
Research, Research, Research

Do a search on the internet for Full- time RVing and you will come up with a wealth of information. I put in Full-time RV and came up all kinds of interesting sites. There is a wealth of information on the internet!

When my research into Solo RVing and Workamping began in earnest; I signed up with Workamper News on their website www.workamper.com. I also signed up to receive the daily hotline. I read the ads about Adventureland in Iowa and this sounded like a great place to start my Workamping experience. It was October and I would not be able to work for them until the spring. I still had a lot to do to get ready for my new life, but needed the security of a promised job. This gave me something to look forward too and helped me realize that it could all come true. So I sent in my application.

They called me and set up an interview at an RV show that would be held in Mercedes Texas in January. I still had doubts about myself at the time so I was worried I would not be hired. However it did give me the hope I needed.

I highly recommend Workamper News to anyone that wants or needs to work, while they RV. For me it was a lifesaver. I have found all except one of my jobs through Workamper News. My awesome applicant resume on the workamper news website has generated offers of work for me. I must say that the jobs advertised for singles are somewhat limited. This is a form of discrimination in the Workamping world. A lot of the Workamper jobs advertised, are for couples. This is usually because the employer has a limited number of campsites, to devote to workampers. I do understand but I don't have to like it! Whenever I am hired, I let my employer know that I appreciate them hiring a single person. I also work hard to fulfill any contract I have with an employer and make sure I give the job 110%, so they will be willing to hire another single workamper.

Make sure when you take a Workamping position that you understand the job you are being hired to do. It is best to get your job description in writing. There is nothing worse than to find out after you get on the job that it requires more than you bargained for. One good thing about my RV lifestyle is the jobs are not permanent positions. I am only there for a short time! My jobs so far have lasted anywhere from seven weeks to seven months. My employers know I have wheels under my home. While I could hook up and pull out at any time, I have so far always fulfilled my contracts. I have found that a positive friendly attitude and a can do spirit, go a long way. I go into a job knowing I am not there to tell my employers how to run their business. I am there to help. I do all in my power to make sure their customers are happy. I find that if I treat people as I want to be treated everyone is happy.

I already belonged to the Good Sam Club. I have been a member for years as they offer a discount on camping at hundreds of campgrounds across the country. I also enjoy reading their magazine, Highways. You can find out more about Good Sam at: www.goodsamclub.com. The Good Sam website is a wealth of RVing information.

I hold a KOA value card membership. With it you get a discount at all KOAs across the country and you can use their website to apply for jobs at KOA campgrounds. Since I was a teen my family has been staying at KOAs. Someday I hope to actually work at one. They are always without exception neat, clean, friendly, and safe. It is a rare thing for me not to feel safe in a campground. Your neighbors are usually only a few feet on either side of your home and most are fine folks. If you need help all you have to do is give out a good shout. For more information on KOAs, go to: www.koa.com.

Just this last year I also joined Passport America. It is a club that offers half price camping. I was a little skeptical about recouping my membership fee, but must admit, it paid for itself. There is not always a Passport America campground on my route. I do stay at them whenever possible. Last summer I worked for Yellowstone General Stores in Yellowstone National Park. I used my Passport America card on the way there and after I left. By the time I got back to Texas I was thankful I made the investment. Most nights I paid between $11 and

$15 for my Passport America campsites. Without the card I would have been paying $22 to $30 a night. Check them out at: www.passportamerica.com.

There are numerous RV clubs out there and all have benefits. As you travel you will find what works best for you and your lifestyle. The ones mentioned above are the ones I have found most useful for me. The bottom line here is to do your research and decide what is right for you. Whether a club that offers discount camping is right for you, very much depends on how much time you actually spend out traveling. With me, I usually spend only about a month total a year in actual travel. I spend part of every year parked in my brother's driveway while I visit family and friends. I spend more time at my work campsites than traveling. It usually takes me less than a week to get to my destination for my next job. However I have learned to slow down and enjoy the trips. So now I don't rush from place to place. I took over 2 weeks to get back to Texas from Yellowstone last summer. It is amazing what you can see if you allow time to enjoy! Before I was not comfortable traveling long distances alone.

Now I have learned that if you just take it one day at a time it does not seem so daunting. My average day on the road is only about 250 miles. Some days I travel further others less! I don't do anything in a hurry! I do plan my days so I am off the road well before dark. I have no desire to be out on the road at night. I also try to travel on secondary roads whenever possible. While the interstates are nice and will get you to your destination they don't appeal to me. I would much rather see small town America. This is a beautiful country we live in and to rush by on the interstate does not do it justice. When I travel through small town America I have to wonder about the people that choose to live there. What are their lives like? You can see their pride in their community by the way all the homes and yards are neat and clean! Every community is unique in its own special way.

When I first started out, I needed the security of arriving at my destination! I was also not financially able to afford long periods of time traveling. It is much cheaper to stay in one place than to constantly move. I have learned that with some planning I can have a wonderful trip as I travel to my next job. I have averaged working 9 months out of each year. The other three months are all mine! Now what kind of regular job would allow you to take a three month vacation?

I recommend reading all you can about Full timing before you run out and buy an RV and hit the open road. It sounds like a dream life but just like any other lifestyle it has its ups and downs. For me the ups far out way the downs.

If you already have an RV and have taken vacations in it, you are one step ahead. I read everything I could find on the internet and even purchased a book on Full time RVing. The book I bought, and highly recommend is: Complete Guide to Full-time RVing by Bill and Jan Moeller. It really helped me feel comfortable about hitting the road. It is reassuring to know others are out there doing what you dream of doing, even if they are doing so, as a couple. There are a lot of singles out here. I find that in most campgrounds the employees are not surprised to find that I am alone. They get a fair number of singles. I stopped at a campground in Kansas last summer and the owner asked me if I was headed to a women's singles rally. He said he had a number of ladies pass through headed to the rally. With campground employees we are not an oddity. Now I can't say that about the general population. It is not unusual for people to watch me when I set up or break camp. I get kind of tickled as I am their entertainment! While camped near Dallas last fall I was setting up and a man kept watching me. I was really surprised he did not come over and offer to help! He seemed so fascinated by the whole process! In that same park as I was hooking up to leave a man stopped to talk! He said he had walked by earlier walking his dog. He would have offered to help but he did not realize I was alone. By the time he stopped I had the truck hooked up to the trailer and was putting the equalizer bars on. He was impressed that I did it all alone! Boy some people have a pretty low impression threshold! Another time I had spent a couple of days in North Platte Nebraska. When I was breaking camp I noticed an older couple in a Class B also getting ready to leave. We ended up leap frogging each other on the interstate all morning. When I pulled into my campground for the night I found they were there just ahead of me. When I went in the office they were just finishing getting checked in. The man said "Weren't you in our campground last night?" I said "I sure was". He went on and on about how impressed he was at the way I handled my rig. I could tell he was embarrassing his wife. The young lady behind the counter and I had a good laugh when his wife finally pulled him out of there! Talk about giving me a boost! My self esteem goes up every time I run into someone with this opinion of what I do. It really is no big deal but it makes me feel good to know others think it is.

Chapter 3
Deciding what RV is right for you.

A large part of my research was into RVs, what I could afford and what I would feel comfortable living and traveling with. There are many different kinds on the market today. There are just as many different folks living in nearly every kind of RV.

I have seen people living in truck campers! For me this would be way too confining. In case you don't know, a truck camper fits in the bed of a pickup. Now don't get me wrong, these are great for getting to remote areas and are easy to handle. The only real difference they make in your driving is they can be a little top heavy. If I ever make that dream trip to Alaska I might just buy one of these little beauties for the trip and resell it when I get back to the lower 48. But to live in one full time would just not work for me.

I have also known several ladies that lived full time in a Class B motor home. These are the small van type motor homes. They usually come with everything including a bath.

However here again as nice as they are and as easy as they are to drive I couldn't live in one. Everything in a Class B is usually pretty small and the dinette table most likely will double as your bed. Driving one of them is no different than driving a full size van.

Then there are the Class C motor homes. Now we are getting into real livability. These motor homes are built on a truck chassis. While the ones with no slide out, still feel a little cramped for me these Motor homes are big enough to be called Home. Most of them also have what it takes under the hood to pull a small car.

Next there is the Class A motor home. I have a number of friends that live in these wonderful monsters of the road. They are the big bus type motor homes you see on the roads and in every campground in America. They are great if you have the money to afford one and what it takes to pilot one down the highway. I can not afford to buy a Class A myself. However I really do not desire one as I do not want to have to take care of two engines. Now you might unhook a Class B or a Class C and take it to the grocery store but no way would you drive your Class A around doing errands. So, you would at least have to tow a car.

For me I soon narrowed my search down to either a travel trailer or 5th wheel. A travel trailer is hooked up by a hitch at the bumper of your tow vehicle. A 5th wheel is attached to a hitch in the bed of a truck. I already had a ½ ton truck that was rated to pull up to 8,000 lbs. so that narrowed my search even further. Now dealers will tell you that a lot of 5th wheels can be towed by ½ ton pickups. Don't just take their word for it. While most are honest they also don't know what your truck is rated to pull. I can't tell you often enough how important it is to consider weight. You don't want to get in a situation where your truck does not have what it takes to get you up the next hill or stop in a reasonable amount of time. Besides that you can do major damage to the engine and transmission of your tow vehicle by towing more weight than it is rated to pull.

Bottom line, before you commit to your new full time home, do your research and don't let anyone pressure you into something you don't feel is right for you. If possible go to RV shows in your area. Visit RV dealerships and go through every kind of RV that interests you. Ask questions! If possible; talk to people that own each different style of RV. Hey, most of us love to talk about our RVs! I am now living in my second travel trailer since I hit the road. When I started out I did so in such a rush and with so little purchase power that I decided to upgrade my RV when I got the chance. This last time when I went looking at RVs I had a wish list of important things to me! Your list may be different than mine but just for a reference here is mine:

A water heater that works on either propane or Electricity. I really would not live without one of these again. I usually have my water heater running on Electric. However if you are dry camping all you have to do is switch it to Propane and you have hot water! I use electricity most of the time for mine because I don't have to refill my propane as often that way. One word of caution before turning it on make sure your water heater is full. If you turn it on while the tank is empty it will burn out the element. Usually this is not a problem unless you have drained your water heater for some reason. Also make sure your Water heater turns on at a switch inside your RV. Trust me; you do not want to have go outside to light the pilot light on your water heater. The trailer my ex-husband and I owned did not have an electronic ignition or work on electric. I had to go out to light the water heater with a match. Try doing that a few times on a rainy and windy day!

Enough room on my kitchen counter for workspace and my dish drainer. I have seen some RVs that barely had room to set a can of beans on the counter! If you cook at all you need counter space.

A walk around bed…No bed that is jammed against a wall for me. It is a nightmare for me to try to make up a bed that is up against a wall.

A large slide out: My sofa and dinette are in a large slide and it makes the trailer much roomier. Next time, I would really like to have a slide out in my bedroom too! Talk about high living!

Inside my Jayco 28FKS

A refrigerator that works on Propane or Electric

Some people use the propane when traveling. I have not found this necessary and I consider it dangerous. However the Propane sure comes in handy if for some reason you have a power failure. Or you decide to dry camp for a day or two.

A good size shower Some RVs have tubs with seats in them and they make it very cramped for taking a shower. Mine does have a tub however there is not a seat in it so there is plenty of room!

An easy chair: I admit it; mine did not come with one! But there was room for one. Now I have purchased a chair and no more sitting on the couch for me. Now I just use my couch for the occasional nap, a guest bed and for guests to sit on!

A separate bathroom: for some reason it disturbs me to have the bathroom and bedroom altogether. This is not uncommon in RVs! I looked at many trailers and 5th wheels that I liked until I discovered that the shower and sink were in the bedroom. The potty usually has its own little closet! I may live alone but I still prefer an enclosed bath.

A pantry: Okay you got me again; my current trailer does not have one. My first trailer did and I must say I miss it.

Leveling jacks: I would not have an RV without them! These are essential; you don't want your RV to move when you walk across the floor.

EZ Lube wheels: With these I can lubricate the wheel bearings myself. The manufacturer still recommends having the bearings pulled and inspected. However between times I can grease them myself.

Ducted Air Conditioner: The ones sticking through the ceiling with no vents are just too noisy for me, and the air all blows in one place. My first Trailer had this kind and it pointed right at my bed! So you are cold if you are right in front of it but other areas of your home are hot! Ducted air disperses the air evenly throughout the RV.

Ample storage As you shop around for a home on wheels, pay close attention to things like closets and storage areas. Remember, this will be your home, you need storage! If there is not enough closet space for your clothes, what will you do with them? You also need storage space for everything you need in your kitchen. As you look, think about, where will I keep my shoes? What will I do with extra sheets, pillows and blankets, when not in use? Where will I store my Christmas decorations? Yes, I travel with a 6 foot slim line Christmas tree and decorations. The tree stores under my sofa and the decorations are under one of my dinette seats.

My Christmas tree

If something is important enough to include it in your new life on wheels, you will have to figure out where to put it. Where will you put a trash can or your dirty clothes? When I purchased my current trailer I found a 5th wheel I really liked. However I realized it did not have any drawers in the kitchen. I could not figure out where I would put my flatware or utensils. So I ended up not getting it.

This was my list and I used it as a guide line when I was looking. It is rare to find just exactly what you want but the closer you come the happier you will be with your choice!

You don't have to buy new! There are usually a lot of gently used RVs on the market. I considered both in my searches. The first one I bought was used and it was a good one. Weight is important no matter which type of RV you intend to use. Before you buy a 5th wheel or travel trailer check to see what your tow vehicle is rated to pull. Be sure you match the RV to your tow vehicle. When I started out I had a 1999 Ford F150 with a 5.4 V8 that was rated to pull 8,000 lbs. My first travel trailer was a used 26 foot 2002 Kiwi Too by Jayco that weighed less than 5,000 lbs empty.

My truck and trailer at Adventureland

Only you can decide what you will be happy with. For me the travel trailer works well. My ex-husband and I owned several travel trailers over the years and I was most familiar with this type of RV. So it is what I am most comfortable with. I have thought about buying a 5th wheel or motor home and may do so sometime in the future. But for now I am happy with my choice. If you end up choosing a motor home you will also have to decide what to do about transportation when you are not traveling. Most people pull a vehicle to use when set up in an RV park. The most common tow vehicle I see is a Saturn, but I have seen just about every car and some trucks being towed. By the way, in RV terms the tow vehicle is called a Toad. A motor home can not back up with a Toad attached. That toad will be all over the place if you try. You still have to consider the weight of the Toad because even Motor homes can be over taxed by weight. Be sure your Motor home is rated to pull a toad safely. Don't rely on the salesman at the lot to know, check the owner's manual yourself! You want to be able to go down the road safely!

My second trailer is a 2006 Jayco Jay Flight 28FKS that weighs 6,200 lbs empty. It has a front kitchen and a rear bedroom. While it is not totally my dream home it is very comfortable and I am for the most part happy with it. I have also upgraded my truck to a 2005 Ford F250 with a 5.4 V8. My F150, while within its towing capacity, just felt a little too light with my heavier trailer behind it. With the F250 I hardly know the trailer is back there.

My Jayco Jay Flight and F250 Truck

I must say some RV parks have begun to restrict the age of the RVs they let stay. To tell you the truth if they are that selective I don't want to stay there anyway. I love walking through an RV park and seeing a variety of different year, make and models of RVs.

Living in the RV world is like being in a whole other world. You may live in a small 19 foot 10 year old travel trailer and your next door neighbor may live in a brand new Class A motor home. I have friends that live in both and they are all good friends! We are all part of the full timing RV family we treat each other as equals and a lot of the time work side by side. We all have similar interest. We love the outdoors and being able to hit the open road any time we want! No matter what part of the country you come from or what your socio-economic background is, you are still part of the RV family.

I work because I need to make a living to support my life on the road. Some of my friends work just because they want to. The truth is even if I did not have to work I think I still would, because I meet so many neat people Workamping. Besides I get tired of my own company!

Chapter 4
Decision, Decisions!

Another biggie is what to do with your home and all your stuff! If you own a home you will have to decide whether to sell it. That is a decision only you can make for yourself. There are a number of pros and cons. For me even if I had a choice I believe I would have sold it anyway. You will have the upkeep for the house whether you are there most of the time or not. You will also have to pay someone to mow the lawn and water the plants at the least. Also, security is a problem when a home is empty. It is not hard for thieves to figure out when no one is home for months on end. You will also have to continue to pay the taxes, insurance, and utilities. However, for some people, they need the security and roots to come home to. Only you know what is right for you. I know people that have kept their home until after they tried the full-time experience for a year or so then decided to let go of their house. If you sell your house, then you have to decide what to do with the things that you just are not ready to let go of. You will have to find some place to store anything you decide you can't part with. Lots of people rent storage for this purpose. For me I let my ex have the furniture and appliances so it left me very little to have to deal with other than small stuff. I spent most of October, November, and December sorting thru 30 years of clutter. My ex-husband rarely threw any thing away nor did he let me! So we had lots of stuff that we might need someday! I had a garage sale at least once a month! Yes, I lived in Texas so this is possible even in the winter. I ended up keeping very little. I have a large quilt box and an old trunk stored in my brothers garage. There were just a few family things that I could not part with. I also went ahead and gave things to family and friends that I knew they would enjoy. They all said the same thing "if you every want it back it is yours". I get pleasure in knowing they are enjoying my stuff. I also had to sort through hundreds of photos we had taken over the years. I rarely go anywhere without a camera. That was really hard for me. I managed to consolidate down to one large photo album that travels with me. Now I take digital pictures and store them on my computer and on Yahoo.com. I also use my photos as my screensaver. It is neat all the good memories that come up with each picture that flashes up on the screen.

Then you have to start considering what you take with you on your new adventure. You don't want to overload your new home with useless stuff! I met one woman that had moved into a 5th wheel with all the clutter from her previous life. I must admit she was a brave soul as she sold her home, bought a big truck and a 5th wheel and hit the road even though she had never camped at all ever! Her 5th wheel was so overloaded that I don't know how she had pulled it all the way from the east coast to Big Bend in Texas! She told me she was sorting and throwing out as she traveled. I cautioned her to get rid of as much as she could as soon as possible. She told me she had already gotten rid of a bunch. Her 5th wheel was so cluttered it was hard to find a place to sit! She told me she had a cat but I never saw it! This lady was doing things backwards….get rid of the clutter in your life first then move into your home on wheels. If you just can't part with the stuff maybe you should reconsider, a life on wheels may not make you happy!

There are options and you will just have to decide what is right for you. It is possible to rent or lease your house out. Then you would have it to come home to someday, but you would most likely have to hire someone to oversee it. Most people just find owning a house while Full-timing is too much of a burden.

If you sell your home and move into an RV I hope you will have a few weeks to make the move. This will give you time to adjust to downsizing! Some people can not buy their RV until after they get the money for their home. This can make the move more difficult as you would have to put your stuff in storage first then live with someone else or in a motel while you wait. Ideally, you want to get your RV and move into it over several weeks. Moving is never an easy job and moving from a large house into an RV can be a real challenge for most folks. It can be done and it is a real freeing experience in the long run. It is amazing how stuff can weigh a person down!

Chapter 5
Getting my first travel trailer

I had an unusual circumstance when I started my Workamping experience. All in one day we got an offer on our house and I was offered a Workamping job. I had applied for a job I saw advertised on the Workamper news Hotline. So as I did not even have an RV I had to go buy one, pack it, finish getting the stuff I wanted to keep out of the house and hit the road in about 4 days! Most of you won't have to act so quickly. I had been surfing the web looking at RV's so I did have the advantage of knowing where to start. I headed off to the dealer's lot where I had found a travel trailer that looked like it might work for me. I had located it on www.rvsearch.com. I ended up making the deal for the Kiwi Too but had to return to Ft. Worth the next day to sign the papers and pick it up. It was about a hundred miles one way from my home to the dealer. I lived near Mexia in central Texas. I hurried home and started putting all the things I was to take with me near the front door. I hardly slept that night as I worked as long as possible. I also had the added burden of packing up my keepsakes to be taken to my brother's house. It was hectic, fun, exciting, and scary all at the same time. The next day I went back and picked up my new home. The dealer had prepped it for me and walked me through the workings of everything. Most dealers will do this. Be sure and ask questions if in doubt about how things work. And by all means read the manual! There is a wealth of information in there. Let them show you how to hook it up to your tow vehicle then have them watch you as you do it yourself!

It was 5 o'clock and raining as I left Ft. Worth. I must say I handled it like I had been pulling that trailer for years. I was really proud of myself and figured if I could do that the first time on the road, I could go anywhere. You have to use your outside mirrors. My new truck has mirrors that extend for towing. They are wonderful large mirrors with big spot mirrors at the bottom. Remember you are pulling extra length, height, and weight. Don't do anything in a hurry. It will take longer to stop and you must make wider turns. I drive about 60 mph when pulling my trailer on the highways. I feel that any faster is just not safe for me! After a few days out on the roads it is almost as comfortable as just driving my truck.

That evening, I called my brother as I was getting home so he could come help me back in to my driveway. When backing a trailer it is important to remember if the back of the truck is turning left the trailer will go right and if the back of the truck is going right the trailer will go left. It takes a little practice but it is not too hard. Slow and easy is the best way to back. I have also found that most places I stay only a night or two, I have pull thrus. If I am going to be someplace long term I usually have to back in, but someone from the office or a campground escort is usually available to help. Don't be afraid or too proud to ask for help. I must admit once, I had help that was worse than if I had done it solo. But this is the exception. I do always get out and look the site over before I back in. However I find it helps to have someone at the back of the trailer to keep me from running over anything. It also saves me having to get in an out of the truck a bunch to check the position of the trailer.

Chapter 6
Things you will need

So, now what to take on the road? Remember this will be your Home. So you need to take everything that will make your life comfortable without overloading your RV. Here I am going to give you a list to consider. My main supplier of camping supplies is Camping World. The website for them is www.campingworld.com.

These all apply no matter what type of RV you buy. I will start with the outside stuff and work my way in.

Water hoses: I have 3 white hoses a 10', 25' & 50' for my potable water. I also have a green hose for use with my sewer tank clean out. You want white for your water because they are made for potable water and you must be able to distinguish them from hoses you use for other purposes.

Insulation for Hoses: I cover my water hose in the winter so it does not freeze. I use foam pipe insulation that you can get at any Hardware store. I head south every winter, so I am usually not in sub freezing weather very long. However as with this winter it does freeze and sometimes it stays that way for awhile. I did find the insulation helpful while in Yellowstone, as I was camped at nearly 8,000 feet. It was not uncommon to have freezing temperatures at night.

Water Pressure regulator: This is a must…by the way it goes on the faucet end! You don't want to blow the water pipes out in your RV because the water pressure is too high.

Tire pressure gauge: Before every trip make sure your tires are properly inflated. The PSI is on the sidewall of the tires or in your owner's manual. This is one of those jobs I really don't enjoy but it is necessary.

Air compressor: Having one of these is easier than going to a service station and trying to get your rig close enough to air up your tires. I bought a small 2 gallon compressor and it works great. I plug it into the outside electric outlet on my trailer.

Wheel chocks: Always chock the tires when you stop for the night and BEFORE you unhook from your truck!!!!!!! You don't want to watch your home roll down a hill! Even if it seems flat and level use wheel chocks!

Levels: My RV dealer installed two of these; one on the front and one on the side of my trailer. It is important that your RV is level. Everything will work better and you won't roll off the bed!

Leveling Blocks: Not all campsites are level so sometimes you will need to drive your rig up on blocks on one side or the other. I also use these under my leveling jacks to keep from having to crank them so far down.

Wheel covers: These will help protect your RV tires from weather rot. The sun can degrade tires over time.

Jack: I purchased a 2 ton hydraulic jack. Big enough for any job I would care to tackle!

Lug Wrench: I have a four way lug wrench. Thank God I have never had to use it! But I have it just in case the occasion should arise.

Electrical adapters: I have an adapter that goes from 50 amps down to 30 amps and one for 30 down to 20. I try not to use them but sometimes you just have to because the campground does not have a matching receptacle for your plug in.

My RV requires a 30 amp receptacle but some use 50 amps.

Extension cords: I have a heavy duty 30 amp cord for when the electrical box is off in the woods such as it was during my summer in Yellowstone. I also carry varying lengths of 20 amp cords for attaching lights outside.

Tool box: I carry a set of screwdrivers, tape measure, a small set of socket wrenches, a pair of needle nose pliers, regular pliers, vise grips, channel lock pliers, hammer, and a cordless screwdriver along with various nuts, bolts and screws, and a few small nails. Oh, and last but not least, duct tape! Let's face it, I am no carpenter but occasionally something needs repaired.

Rope: I have found that if I attach a rope to my awning loop I don't have to dig out the wand every time I want to raise or lower the awning. (Thanks for the tip Margaret!) Be sure and take the rope off before you travel again.

Sewer Hose: I carry several various lengths, as not all situations are equal. I have two 20 foot lengths and one 10 foot. I also carry a rubber doughnut for the drain end of the hose as well as an elbow. I have found sometimes the elbow works great and at other campgrounds the rubber donut works better. You want as tight a seal as possible. I also have 3 connections to join hoses together.

RV Hydro Flush: This attaches between the sewer hose and the sewer connection on your RV. Mine is a clear plastic and it works great for back flushing the black tank. I don't use it every time I drain my tanks; however I use it on average about once a month. It helps to keep the tank clean. Some higher end RV's come with a built in tank flushing system.

Sewer Hose Support: I use a slinky type. When you drain your tanks you want the stuff to flow downhill out of the hose into the sewer. If it is just laid out on the ground, as I see frequently the hose will not always drain properly.

Disposable Gloves: Let's face it you don't enjoy working with a sewer and you sure don't want that stuff on your bare hands. YUK! Actually, it rarely happens that you get actual sewage on your hands because if connected properly it all drains away. However you are touching the hoses the sewage passed through and there may be residue even if you don't see it. Wear the gloves and dispose of them properly so you don't spread bacteria! I have noticed some people wear work gloves for this job but I don't believe this is a good idea. Because whatever the glove touches after handling the sewer hose will then have bacteria transferred on to it!

Large Plastic Tote: I keep all of my sewer connections, my hose support and a 20' length of sewer hose in one of these. Most RVs come with a place for sewer hoses in the bumper. But you will find there just is not room for everything in there and some of the connections won't fit. A large plastic tote with a tight lid dedicated to sewer parts keeps everything contained. (Thanks for the tip Johnny!)

Bungee Cords: You can't have too many of these in all sizes. I use a small one to attach my sewer cap to the RV so it does not bang against the underside of the trailer in the wind. I also secure my electrical pigtail to my truck with a small bungee. It is no fun if your electrical connection comes loose from your truck while traveling and you have to repair or replace it. Besides if it is not connected your trailer lights and brakes will not work!

Awning tie downs: If you are going to leave your awning out unattended you need to make sure it is tied down. The wind can come up unexpectedly and do major damage to it and your RV if it comes loose. It is best to take it in before you leave for the day.

Lawn Chair: I carry 2 one for me and another for anyone that might drop by for a visit.

Folding Table: I carry a folding card table and a small TV tray type table that I can use inside or out.

Outdoor Rug: I use a turf rug that looks like green grass. It helps me keep from tracking a lot of dirt and debris into my home. Some campgrounds restrict the use of these. I am always careful not to cover grass as it will die if covered too long. I use a Karpet Tack kit I bought at Camping World to secure it so it won't blow around.

Ladder: I carry a ladder so I can get up to see on my slideout before I bring it in. If you are parked under a tree this is important. As you do not want to damage the slide or side of your RV with broken tree limbs or other debris when you bring it in. I also use the ladder when I wash the trailer.

Folding step stool: I am short so I need a little step up occasionally. I use mine both outside and inside.

Extra Step: I need an extra step below my RV steps most of the time. My travel trailer is pretty high and has three steps. However, as I said before I am short and usually I need a fourth step. This is especially true, if I have to put blocks under the tires on the door side of my trailer. For the past two years I have used an exercise step. It is light weight and just the right height. My little dog also appreciates the extra step.

The list seems long already but it is not as bad as it seems. I did not purchase everything at once. I have added things as I have gone along. Now I don't know how I would get along without any of these things.

I will move on to the list for inside. I am going to try to cover all the important stuff. Even though I am sure you are smart enough to realize you will need most of it.

Dishes: I refuse to eat off of paper plates all the time! Let's face it I live here and like my comforts! A drippy paper plate is not my idea of enjoyable dining. When I moved into my RV

I already had a set of Corelle Christmas dishes. I use them everyday of the year. Someday I might find some I like better, and company might think it is a little odd but it works for me. I have only broken one plate and it was in my microwave not while traveling. I suggest a service for 4 as you might have guests. If you have more people coming to dinner either use paper or ask each guest to bring their own plate and flatware. It can be fun to see all the different patterns. As for serving dishes remember it is just you and you won't need a lot of large ones. I have several small ones and one large one I use when I attend pot lucks. I also carry 3 nesting plastic bowls I use to mix things.

Flatware: As with the Dishes I suggest a service for 4. You can use only one set at a time.

Utensils: You will need the usual things you most commonly use in your kitchen now. Just don't over do it and carry all that stuff you have only used once or twice! Face it all our houses had drawers that were full of utensils that sounded like a good idea but really were no great help!

Groceries: Okay we all eat. Admit it you do too. Things you cook and eat now, you will continue to enjoy on the road. Just don't overload your cabinets when you head down the road. I have found it to be a real adventure to go to local grocery stores. It is amazing to me how different they can be in different areas of the country. I usually carry just enough groceries to get me from my starting point to my destination then stock up when I arrive. I do stock up on things that are local favorites that I know will be more expensive at my destination or maybe not available at all. Otherwise I try to let my cabinets run pretty bare before a trip. If you are going to a remote area be sure and stop at the last large town to stock up. Traveling over 70 miles one way just to buy groceries is not my idea of a great time. Believe me I have had to do this several times and you really want to stock up before you get to the boonies!

Linens: I use cloth napkins most of the time.....one of my little luxuries and they don't weigh much, so I carry 8 of them. I also have several kitchen towels, dish cloths, and pot holders. For the bath I carry 6 towels, 3 hand towels and a supply of wash cloths. I carry 3 sets of sheets as my bed, sofa and dinette all make beds. I also carry 3 blankets and 6 pillows. My home may be small but my family and friends are always welcome and I want to be prepared if someone wants to spend the night. It would be very cramped for many people to stay for an extended time but several days can be fun.

Toaster or Toaster Oven: I traveled a year without this but I found one to be invaluable. As anyone who has ever used a small RV oven knows, they are less than desirable for making toast.

Dish Drainer: Okay I admit I am lazy when it comes to drying dishes. I purchased a small one at the local discount store. It sits on the counter next to my sink. This is also something to keep in mind when buying your RV. Most of the time counter space is minimal too non existent. It is one of the things I considered important when looking for an RV. I would not buy an RV without room for my dish drainer! Also be careful not to get a tiny dish drainer that fits in one of these small RV sinks. They just don't hold enough.

Paper towel Holder: How would we live without these little gems? I have one that stands on a counter or table top.

Pots & Pans: Yes, you will still have to cook! It all depends on how into cooking you are as to how many and of what quality you want to take. I have RV friends that prefer to eat out most of the time. Others love to cook and spend more time cooking than when they were in a regular house. It is up to you but don't take pots or pans that you would rarely use. It just is not worth giving up the room or the extra weight involved.

TV: I admit it I am a TV junky! I love watching TV…it keeps me company. I purchased 2 LCD flat screen TVs a 15" for the bedroom and a 20" for the living area. I chose them because they are light weight. Yes, I am on the weight thing again. I put a couple of eye hooks in the wall near my living room TV and use a bungee hooked to them to secure it for travel. My bedroom TV has to be taken down and be stored for travel.

Satellite Dish: Yes, I travel with a satellite dish. As I said before I do like my TV. I use Dish network but others use Direct TV. When I was in Yellowstone I would not have had any TV without my dish as the area is so remote. Usually you can pick up locals with the antenna attached to the roof of your RV. In some cases campgrounds offer cable TV connections.

Setting up the Dish is not always easy but so far I have managed the task with success. All you have to do is go to the setup menu for the satellite on your TV and enter your present zip code. The screen will give you the coordinates for setting your dish. Mine sits on a tripod either at the rear or front of my trailer. It is good that it is portable because if I don't have a clear view of the southwest sky, I can move it. I use a digital compass to point it to the desired location. I have to use my sockets and a wrench to adjust the elevation and Skew of the dish. If I get the settings just right and it is level it works great! Occasionally weather disrupts the signal but this is rare. I have a DVR with my dish so I can record programs while I am at work and watch them any time. I LOVE IT.

Computer: I don't think I can live without my computer. I do everything on it from keeping in touch with family and friends to keeping my financial records. And yes I play computer games for entertainment. I started out with a

desk top model but was later able to buy a
Notebook. When I had the Desk top it took up
all the room on my dinette so I had to eat off a
TV tray. Now with the small one it can go
where ever I am. I still have a large multi
function printer. I keep it stored under my
dinette bench when not in use. My computer has
Wifi and I have found it is easier all the time to
find hot spots. A lot of RV parks have Wifi
these days and with some it is even free!

806-9125
806-9265

② Bennett
Plumbing
Father &
Son

593-0214
Bobby's Cell

     I use a web based email account so it is
easy to access my email from any computer.
Most libraries allow computer use these days
also. I use www.yahoo.com and
www.iwon.com for my email. There are others
out there so all you have to do is search the web
to find a free email account that will suit you. I
do have a modem and have from time to time
used People Pc but only when I am hooked up
to a land telephone line. When I was out at Big
Bend the first time they did not have Wifi so I
got a telephone just so I could have internet.
Then last summer in Yellowstone I also had a
land line phone. This is getting to be a rarer
occurrence as Wifi becomes more widely used.

THOUSAND TRAILS PARK (RV)

GPS System: While this is not exactly necessary it sure makes traveling solo easier. One of the things I found hard when I started out was not having any one to read a map for me! I would plot out my route the night before and write all the highways and turns on a piece of paper. This was helpful but reading while driving is not exactly what I would advise. Last Year I invested in the DeLorme GPS. It came with the GPS and software for my computer. It talks to me and I can talk to it!!!!! I boot my computer up and plot my route in the DeLorme program. Then when I am ready to go I put the GPS on my dash and plug in my headphones and microphone. I purchased a power converter, used to plug my computer into the accessory port on the dash board of my truck. Then off I go with the computer telling me where to turn and when. I set the computer down in the floorboard of my truck and I can glance down to see where I am on the map display. I can ask questions like how far to the next turn and it will answer me! This is just too cool. I got off on the wrong road in Tulsa Oklahoma and if I had not had the GPS I would have had a hard time getting out of there headed the right way! It was raining and there had been a traffic accident and so I missed my turn. I trusted the GPS system and followed the directions it gave me and before I knew it, I was headed in the right direction again. Well worth the $100 it cost me.

Cell phone: I know a few people that travel without one of these but it is my lifeline. I use a plan with no roaming and no long distance. Otherwise I could not afford one! There are lots of companies and plans out there as you all know so chose the one that is right for you. I usually keep my phone on but have found if I don't power it down and back up sometimes my calls will go to voice mail because the system can not find me. By turning it off and back on the nearest tower will locate my phone so when I get a call it will come through. When I am traveling I usually call one of my nieces to let her know where I am heading and what roads I plan to take. Then I call her again when I reach my destination for the night. She worries about her Aunt Joy when she knows I am on the road. This way keeps her from worrying too much and gives me the security of someone knowing where I am. One time I was not able to get cell phone service when I arrived at my stop for the night. I was however able to get on the internet using Wifi. So I was able to get a message to my niece that I had arrived safely.

Telephone: I carry a land line phone for those times when I want "regular" phone. So far I have used it twice as described above. I also carry lots of telephone line and a coupler so I can join two lines. Sometimes it is a long way to the telephone hook up!

Books: I love books! It was one of the hardest things I had to do when I left my large supply of hard back books behind. Now most of the books I have are paper backs. The ones I get for leisure reading I pass on after I read them. I exchange them for others at campground exchanges or used bookstores or give them away. Now all my books are soft covers (lighter) and most have to do with RVing.

I have in my not so extensive library now: the current Trailer Life Directory, The Official Good Sam Club RV Road Atlas, Mountain Directories East and West, Trailer Life's RV Repair and Maintenance Manual, National Audubon Society Field Guide to North American Birds, and Women's Devotional

Bible. In addition I have one book on CD: <u>The</u> <u>Woman's Guide to Solo RVing</u>. There are lots of good books out there you just have to find the ones that will help you the most. When I was up in the Des Moines area I used the Altoona Public Library. It was great about loaning books to people that worked for Adventureland. **Clothes:** I know you all wear clothes! But some people have been known to hit the RV road with their whole wardrobe in tow! Trust me you won't need a bunch of dressy clothes. In case you have not noticed clothes are heavy! Don't take all the dresses or suits in your wardrobe even if there is room in your RV's closets, which I doubt. Keep a couple of nice dresses or suits in case you go to church or a wedding or a funeral. Otherwise your new lifestyle just will not require more formal wear. You will find yourself most likely in jeans and T-shirts or as I prefer Polo shirts. Anything casual that is easy to wash and wear is the norm. But don't over do it on these either. There are washers and dryers at nearly every campground I have stayed at! About 10 days worth of casual wear should suffice. I do have a heavy winter coat, a lined wind breaker and a blue jean jacket, a rain coat, as well as a couple of sweaters. I also have short and long sleeve shirts about 8 each. At different jobs I have been required to wear either black or Khaki pants so I have 1 each of these as well as a few pair of shorts. Make it a rule that when you bring in a new item of clothing you throw something out! Otherwise before you know it your closets will be bulging and your truck will be straining to get up the hills!

Shoes: Yes, I know for some people this is a difficult hurdle to jump. I have a couple of pairs of dress shoes, 2 pair of boots (one rubber and the other winter), a pair of sandals, and 2 pair of tennis shoes. My jobs have required either black or white tennis type shoes for the most part. So I have one of each. Oh and I almost forgot a pair of warm slippers! If you work where you have to stand most of your shift be sure to buy the best shoes you can afford! Believe me your feet will thank you.

Jewelry: Keep it simple....flashy is not good when your travel alone. Most of my employers have had guidelines as to what is appropriate and they limit jewelry to a ring on each hand, simple earrings, a watch and a small necklace. I do have some flashy stuff I keep for the occasional dress up occasion but it is all costume jewelry no one would care to steal. It still is pretty to look at and makes me feel dressed up.

First Aid Kit: I have all the usual things you would find in a medicine cabinet. Be sure and take along stuff to keep insects at bay as will as medicine for stings and bites. I have not had much problem with this but it does happen when you spend a lot of time outside. Also take along any prescription medications needed. I would advise you to use one of the chain pharmacies so you can get your prescriptions filled wherever you happen to be!

PERSONAL Stuff: Don't over do it with this but everyone needs things around them to remind them of happy times. I have an old lamp that was my mother's. My brother and great niece rewired it for me and I bought it a new shade that I decorated with beads. It had been in my parent's house most of my life and looks like an old pump with the handle used to turn it on and off! It is special to me and makes my home on wheels feel like home. I also have an old cabbage patch doll that sits on the back of my sofa. Howard Max has been with me a lot of years and does not eat or take up much room. Also I have a picture frame that is about 30 inches square. I filled it with family photos and all I have to do is look up from my chair and my family is smiling down at me. These small touches make my home my very own special place.

Alarm Clock: Okay I said it! When you are working unless you have the late shift you might need one of these dreadful things! I usually wake up before mine goes off but occasionally the obnoxious noise does its job.

Vacuum Cleaner: Most RVs have at least some carpet. You will need one of these like it or not!

Weather Radio: I believe this is a must for anyone living the RV lifestyle. Safety is my number one reason for having one. If there is a bad storm coming you need time to get to a solid building. I have been in some pretty bad storms in my RV and not had a problem but it is better to be prepared to evacuate. If my weather radio says a tornado is headed my way I am out of here!

Chemicals: I have found an enzyme based holding tank chemical to work well. They also do not harm the environment. The main thing with your black holding tank is to make sure you put plenty of water in them after each time you empty the tanks. If you put in at least three gallons of water it will help keep your tank from getting clogged. I use a black streak remover on the outside of my RV when I wash it. Black streaks will appear wherever water runs down the side of your rig. Your owner's manual will advise you on what is best to use on the surfaces inside your RV. In mine I can use most non toxic household cleaners. I also carry Silicone spray for use on my stabilizer jacks to keep them from squealing when I crank them up or down.

Hobby Items: If you have a hobby such as fishing, playing golf or sewing by all means take the stuff you need to continue enjoying the things you love. I have a Solo friend that enjoys quilting. She took the extra easy chair out of her 5th wheel and installed a sewing center. There are ways of incorporating your hobbies into your RV lifestyle. I have camped where there were great fishing streams running right past the campground or on the edge of a pristine golf course. Whatever your hobby is, plan to continue to enjoy it while you live full time in your home on wheels.

Flashlight: I have a heavy Mag-lite flashlight. It is powerful enough to give me a good size light. I also have a small one.

Backpack: I find one of these very useful for a picnic or a day spent hiking. I always carry a few items for first aid and a couple of bottles of water. A Backpack allows me to keep my hands free.

Walking stick: I have a wood walking stick that has a bell attached. The bell is supposed to scare away bears! I find what I call my third leg helpful when I hike. Now they make light weight telescoping walking sticks. They look kind of like ski poles!

Collapsible Cooler: My small collapsible cooler is just right for taking a lunch to work with me.

Grill: Not all campsites come with a grill. I have a gas grill that attaches to a bracket on the outside of my trailer. I love to use it to cook out.

Music: I found out in far west Texas that I could not pick up a radio station. Now I travel with several CD's of my favorite traveling music. Singing to my self is not good!

Suitcase: I do occasionally spend the night away from my home on wheels. I know it is hard to believe someone would take a vacation from this life but it happens. Usually it is Christmas or a holiday and I spend the night with family. Just like any home you will find times when you will be away. Usually it is only for a few days at most. So a small suitcase and an overnight bag is enough. My bags nest together and are kept under my bed until needed.

Fire Proof Box: You will need one of these to keep your important papers in. I have things like insurance papers, birth certificate and passport in mine.

File Drawer: I keep those receipts and papers we all accumulate over the year in one of these. It is a small letter size plastic one. At the end of the year after I file my taxes I clean it out and start all over.

RV Insurance: You need to get Full-time RV insurance. Most people who use their RV's for vacations just add it to their auto insurance. That is okay but as Full-timers we usually have everything we own in our RV's. It is also our home so we need insurance just like someone with a regular home. My Trailer is insured for replacement cost, contents and roadside assistance. I also have a liability policy. If someone should fall and hurt themselves leaving my trailer I am covered. I actually had to use the roadside assistance once. I was out in the Big Bend area and had a flat tire. I called and they sent a man out to fix it for me. He had to travel 78 miles one way! I did not have to pay him one dime, because of my insurance. He pulled the flat tire off my trailer and put the spare on. I signed the invoice and he was on his way. My insurance company was charged $155.

Be sure when you shop for your insurance that you tell the company you live full time in your RV. Not all companies offer full time insurance. I currently use Foremost. In the past I have had Progressive. Good Sam also offers insurance for full timers. I am sure there are others. I pay almost as much for my Trailer insurance as I did my house. But I consider it worth every dime. I will not be left homeless if I lose it.

Chapter 7
How I found my first job and got on the road

Now let's get on with how this all began for me.   My first job was working as a waitress out in the Big Bend area of Texas.

Me on the job at Big Bend Motor Inn Cafe

Talk about jumping into a new life style! I had never lived alone as a workamper much less been a waitress! I found an ad in the Workamper news hotline and applied. They were advertising for a store clerk and also for a waitress. I did not even have an RV yet. I knew without a job I could not get the credit I needed to purchase my home on wheels. With the promise of a job and my good credit I was able to secure the loan for my travel trailer. Our home had not sold so I did not have the cash to buy an RV out right. As I said earlier we got an offer on our home and I got offered the job all in the space of a few hours. I had applied for the clerk job. However when the Manager called he told me that he really needed a waitress more than a clerk. I told him I had never been a waitress. He said if you are willing to learn my wife will be glad to teach you. I was willing and as they say the rest is history! All my ducks were lining up in a neat little row. This is what I had dreamed of. All I had to do was live the dream. When I got back to the house after picking up my new home in Ft Worth it was late in the evening so I could not do much then to get it packed up and ready. I spent another night making lists of things I would need and stacking stuff by the front door. I was as excited about my used trailer as I would have been if it was brand new! It was gently used and most of my family and friends who came to see it, thought it was new.

I once again had the help of my sister-in-law. After I made a trip to the store to buy things I thought I would need. She came home with me and helped me. I would take things to the door of the trailer and she would load them in and put things where she thought they should be. I must admit she did a wonderful job and I could never have made it without her help. I was not just packing for a vacation I was packing for my new life!

I was a little nervous to be heading out on the open road alone. While Big Bend is in Texas it might as well be in another state as it is 600 miles from my home town. This was no little day trip I was embarking on. I was leaving my home and all that was familiar behind. As I set off on the adventure of my life time. I kept telling myself I can do this! When I left home my family and neighbors were there to see me off. They kept asking me if I had this or that and insisted on loaning me a lug wrench, fix a flat, and jumper cables. It was enough to make a woman afraid to pull out of the driveway! With tears in my eyes and my little dog Ellie beside me I did manage to pull out and keep going. My brother and nephew did most of the hooking up of my trailer to my truck, while I finished with last minute things in the house. That was the last time anyone has done this for me. I know I could find help in any campground if I needed it and I do get offers. But I prefer to do it all myself because then I know it is done right.

I spent the first night of my new life as a fulltimer at the KOA in Junction Texas. When I arrived and was escorted to my site I discovered that I did not have a long enough water hose. The connections for my utilities were located near the back of my trailer. While the water faucet and electrical box were near the front of the site! My trailer had come with what they called a starter kit that included toilet paper, sewer hose with connections, tank treatment, and water pressure regulator. The water hose with my starter kit was only 10 ft. long so I went back up to the campground office/store and purchased a longer water hose. I had already purchased a longer sewer hose but it had not occurred to me that my water hose might also be too short. So you can learn from my mistakes. Most campgrounds have a good stock of the most commonly used RV parts and accessories. I found the people at the KOA friendly and helpful. I did not unhook my trailer that night. It just did not seem worth the effort for one night. I also did not hook up the sewer hose.

When I am traveling I do not bother to hook it up every night. My holding tanks do not have much in them when I travel as I dump them when I head out and usually every other day if I am on the move. If I am set up for an extended period of time I dump my Black tank once a week. The grey tank has to be emptied more often as long showers will fill it up quicker. Sometimes I will leave the grey valve open and then close it a day or so before I empty the black tank so I have plenty of grey water to rinse out the sewer hose. With the grey tank what ever works for you is okay. With the black tank…NEVER leave the valve open as this will drain off liquids and leave the solids in the bottom of the tank to become sludge! YUK! Set a day of the week to empty your tanks then you won't have to try to remember when you did it last!

As I arrived in Junction I spotted an easy access Service station. So I knew I could fill up on my way out with no problem the next morning.

I was so excited, exhausted and apprehensive that first night. After getting settled in to our campsite, I took Ellie out for a walk. We had a good long walk and even saw a couple of deer. The campground was so peaceful I could feel myself relax. Yes, I missed everything that was familiar but oh what an adventure I was embarking on. Everything was going to be okay…I could do this!

Chapter 8
Breaking Camp

Let me go through the procedures for breaking camp. They are pretty much the same whether you have a travel trailer, or 5th wheel. You would do a lot of the same things with a motor home but I have very little experience with one so I will just tell what I know. I first get everything inside the trailer secured. Things will bounce around inside so you want to secure all loose items. I do as much of this as possible the night before I move. I take the shade off my lamp and set it in the kitchen sink as well as any house plant. I also take anything on the kitchen counters and store them in cabinets. I take my lamp off my night stand and lay it on my bed as well as my alarm clock. I also take my bedroom TV and place it into the Styrofoam it was originally packed in and put it beside the bed on the floor. I take my big family collage of pictures off the wall so it won't fall off during travel. Anything else that is loose is then put away. I push my living room TV back against the wall and place the bungee across the front of it to hold it in place. My DVD player and dish DVR are both permanently secured with Velcro on the bottom. Then I make sure my TV antenna is in the down and locked position. I have seen people pull out of campgrounds with their TV antenna extended in the upright position and trust me they don't travel well that way! Next I take down my dining room table and lay it on my bed. Then I slide my easy chair between the dinette seats. Next I push the button and pull the slideout of my trailer in. The last thing I do in the trailer is turn my refrigerator to the off position. Some people travel with the propane turned on and the refrigerator working on gas. I consider this dangerous. I have found even in the hot summer time my refrigerator stays cold. When it is really hot outside I use an ice pack or two in the bottom. Ice stays frozen in the freezer. I have found in my travels that things near the front of the trailer move around the least. The closer to the back of the trailer the more likely something is to move in travel.

Then I move to the outside and start my work there. I first dump both holding tanks. The black tank first then the grey one so it rinses out the hose. I then unhook the sewer hose and put it in the tote I carry for that purpose. Then I put the tote in the back of the truck. I throw away the disposable gloves I wear to handle the sewer hose and use a wet wipe to clean my hands. Next I unhook the fresh water hose. I fill my fresh water tank about a third full. This allows me to use my own restroom while traveling and should I need to dry camp I am prepared. I don't travel with the tank full because water weighs 8 pounds a gallon. There is no need to carry more than needed. I place my hose in the big bucket I carry for that purpose. I then unplug from the electrical box. I turn the breaker off at the box while I unplug then turn it back on after I am finished. Then I push the line back up into the side of the trailer and latch down the cover. I then crank up my stabilizer jacks and pick up the blocks under them. I always take them in order so I don't forget one! I store the blocks in the back of my truck in a box I use just for them. This keeps them from rattling around in the bed of the truck. Then I take down my Satellite dish and store it also in the back of my truck. It does not take nearly as long to take it down as it does to set it up. All I have to do is loosen the bolts holding the tripod to the Satellite dish and pull the dish out. Then I fold the tripod and put it and the dish in the bed of my truck. I also make sure my awning is securely locked in place. I use a couple of bungee cords wrapped around the arms just for my peace of mind. This gives it a little more security.

Now if you have a 5th wheel you would use the under storage for all the things I put in the back of my truck. Then I make sure both of my propane tanks are turned off. After that I am ready to start the hookup. I raise the front jack so my trailer tongue is higher than my truck hitch. By the way I usually take my hitch off the truck when I am not traveling. It sticks out a good bit and I don't want some unsuspecting person walking by to run into it! Talk about an ouch! I usually have to get out several times as I back up to make sure the truck hitch is lining up right to the trailer. This gets easier every time I do it. I had a power jack put on the front of my RV so I do not have to use a hand crank. I am now pretty spoiled to doing things the easy way. When the ball of the hitch is under the coupler I lower the trailer. When it is seated I latch it and raise the trailer back up to attach the equalizer bars. Then I hook up the chains, break away brake line and connect the electrical pig tail to the truck receiver. With a 5th wheel it is much the same procedure except you are hooking up in the bed of your truck and there are no chains or equalizer bars to hook up. When you purchase an RV your dealer will show you the proper way to hookup. It only takes a little practice to get comfortable with the procedure and you can and make lots of lists to check off as you move along. Even now when I do something out of the ordinary I will put a check list on my truck steering wheel so I don't forget anything. I find I really don't need the list under ordinary circumstances, as I have a routine I follow. Once my trailer is all hooked up to the truck I remove the wheel chocks and tire covers. Then I am ready to move forward and pick up any leveling blocks. I also do a quick walk around and check that everything is done and that I am leaving nothing behind. If in doubt make a list and check it at least twice. It is much better to be safe than sorry.

Chapter 9
Setting up camp

Setting up camp is pretty much breaking camp in reverse! The only big difference is if you forget to do something it is not such a big deal! I do not always unhook from my truck at night. If it is just a one night stay and I have no plans to go anywhere I leave the truck and trailer hooked together. It is important even if not unhooking for the night that the trailer is level. I check this first and if needed put blocks under the low side. I also check that there is room for my slideout! I don't want to hit anything with it. My slide is 36" so I carry a yard stick in my truck. Before unhooking my trailer I make sure the slide has enough clearance. I also put a mark on my walking stick. All I have to do is put one end against the side of the trailer and make sure nothing is in range of the slide! If I am going to unhook I make sure that the first thing I do is chock the wheels. Even if I don't unhook I usually put at least two wheel chocks in place. I put blocks under the front jack on my trailer as well as under my stabilizer jacks. I have on several occasions found that the hitch on my truck can be higher than my jack alone can raise my trailer. This all depends on your campsite. Some of them are not truly level and this can cause problems. To unhook the trailer I let my jack down and raise the back of the truck and trailer. This takes most of the pressure off the equalizer bars and it is easier to remove them. Then I lower the jack and uncouple the trailer from the hitch. Unhook all the chains and the electrical line and then move the truck forward. Then I am ready to hook up the electric so I can get my refrigerator running again. I also turn one of my propane tanks back on. I hook the appropriate water hose up. Next I put down the stabilizer jacks and then put my slide out. Then Ellie is ready to go back in the trailer. Next I hook up my sewer hose. My trailer has two grey water tanks. One is for the galley and the other for the bathroom. As the galley tank valve is under the trailer where the slide is I open it. I leave it open until I move the slide in again. This way I only have to crawl under the slide once!

Next I go inside and put everything back where it belongs. I am home!

Chapter 10
Traveling with Pets

As I mentioned before, I travel with my little dog Ellie.

She is a good old dog and great company. I know a lot of people that travel with their pets. Some have dogs and others have cats. Some even have both! Dogs are a little more trouble because they have to be walked regularly. No matter the weather they still have to go out. Ellie does not care if it is raining or freezing outside she takes her walks seriously. She thinks she has to sniff every blade of grass to find just the right spot to go!

I discovered our second day on the road that Ellie does not like the windshield wipers on my truck. I had her bed in the floor in front of the passenger seat. As soon as I turned on the windshield wipers a black streak went past my right shoulder. Now she is an old dog as I said and jumping is not her forte. But she jumped up in the seat and over the console into the back seat area of my truck as quick as any young dog could. She wedged herself in between the monitor and printer of my desk top computer. It was a pretty good distance before I came to a road side park and was able to shift things around so she could stay back there comfortably. Now I know she prefers to be a back seat passenger.

Before I start hooking the trailer up Ellie goes into the back seat area of my truck on her bed with a supply of water. It makes her nervous for me to move the trailer up and down if she is still in it. When we arrive at camp she stays in the truck until I have the trailer level and unhooked. If it is too hot out for her to stay in the truck I put her on a leash. Once the trailer is all set up she is happy to be home. It does not seem to matter to her that the outside scenery is different as long as she has the same bed and home she is happy. She also does not like to be in the trailer when I move the slide!

If you decide to travel with a pet be sure they are up to date on all their shots and take a copy of their medical records with you. Should they need a vet it will help for the new one to be able to see what care they have had from their regular Vet. Ellie and I make a visit to her Vet every spring before we head out to our summer job. As we have always wintered in Texas this works out well for us. Pets can be a lot of company when you travel but you must decide if the benefits of having a pet are worth it for you. Ellie is also afraid of storms so I really worry about her when I am working and a storm comes up. I have also been known to stay home with her and forego an outing with friends because I did not want her to be alone when it was thundering. Okay, you got me; I am an old softy when it comes to animals!

My dog is friendly with every person she meets. She thinks everyone in her path is supposed to stop and pet her! She does not understand when she does not get the attention she thinks she deserves. Some people just are not dog people but I can't get her to understand. On the other hand she rarely meets another dog she likes! When we are out walking and someone with another dog approaches I will usually take her in the opposite direction. She growls at every dog she meets! I don't know if she is scared and wants to get her bluff in first or if she truly doesn't like other dogs.

We have had a few problems with people letting their dogs run free in RV parks. If we are approached by a free roaming dog I pick Ellie up and head for home. I don't want her getting into a fight. I really don't think she would hurt another dog but I don't want to take any chances. Most RV parks have rules about pets being on leashes but some people can't seem to obey them. I always pick up after Ellie. I find that plastic grocery bags work great for this. We try to be courteous neighbors and hope other pet owners will be too. The only time Ellie barks is if someone knocks on our door. I asked my neighbors so I could be sure she does not bark if I am not home. They said they never hear a peep out of her. It is no fun to be parked in an RV park and have your neighbor's dog barking all day or night. Cats also make good

RV pets. Some people even walk their cats on leashes. You do have to be careful that they don't escape from your RV but they can be great company. I have a friend that travels with a cat that makes a game of trying to escape from her 5th wheel! She always picks him up and backs down her steps. Then she throws him in the RV and quickly shuts the door! If he escapes, he loves to play catch me if you can. Have you ever tried to catch a cat? With cats you also have to figure out what to do with their litter box. This can be a problem. I know some people that keep the litter box in their shower. Also I have friends that put a cat door in the bottom of a closet and put the litter box there.

Be aware if you do decide to travel with a pet that some campgrounds prohibit pets all together and others have size or breed restrictions. When I make campground reservations I always mention that I travel with my dog. That way the campground employee has a chance to tell me if there are any restrictions. Above all; if you decide to have a pet along for the companionship please obey the park rules. Those that don't obey the rules make it hard on everyone else. We may not always agree with every rule set down by campgrounds but they usually have their reasons based on some past event! It is our responsibility to be courteous and, responsible pet owners. Obey the rules whatever they are, so we can all continue to enjoy our pets and they can enjoy traveling with us.

Chapter 11
Am I lonely?

I am asked all the time how do you do it alone? Don't you get lonely? The answer is yes, sometimes I am very lonely. However I would be lonely if I lived in a regular house and had a regular job! I have found that usually when I am in a new place and meeting new people I have little time to think about my state of living alone. It really is not such a bad thing. I don't have to worry about anyone else! I eat when I am hungry, sleep when I am sleepy and do what I want when I want. I do miss the companionship of having someone with me when I am traveling and seeing new sights. Mainly; because there is no one there to ooh and aah with me. When this Texas gal arrived in Yellowstone National Park last May there was still snow piled beside the road and Lewis Lake was frozen. I was beside myself with joy!

Lewis Lake frozen

God's wonders always amaze me! I am a Christian so I am never truly alone! I have a peace about what I am doing and I know I am in God's will. I can do the things I do because of my faith.

I have made so many friends in the two years that I have been Workamping. It is amazing to me that I now have more true friends than I ever had when I was living in a regular house.

I recently made a trip to Camping world with one of my nieces. As I walked in the door I discovered a friend from my Big Bend Workamping days. My niece was following me as we entered. She thought "Boy Aunt Joy is sure glad to be at Camping World." Because, I went straight to him and gave him a big hug! His wife and I have stayed in touch through email. They had made a trip to the mall where I was working during the Christmas holidays to visit me. I knew he might be there as he was working there part time. However I was not sure so I had not mentioned him to my niece. They were some of my very first Workamping friends and will always be special to me. Email is a wonderful thing! It has allowed me to keep in touch with so many of the great people I have met in my travels. I also pick up my cell phone and call friends to check up on them. It is always fun to hear what someone else is doing and to get caught up on where they are!

It is not unusual for one of my friends to call and say "Hey Joy we are going to be near your area lets get together". When we do get back together after a long separation, it is like we have never been apart because we have so much in common. And we are interested in each others experiences Workamping. When I first started out on my travels I knew no one other than local people. Now I have friends scattered all over the country.

We almost all carry "business" cards with us to give to our Workamping friends. I have a whole collection that grows with every job I have. These little gems are our way of passing our important information such as Telephone #, email address and permanent mailing address to each other. Most of us even have our photos on our cards. In this way we can stay in touch no matter if the miles have separated us.

I must say my first summer job working at Adventureland was one of the most rewarding experiences for me. I met more new friends there and it was good for my soul! There was no reason to be lonely at Adventureland.

Front Gates at Adventureland

They hire hundreds of Workampers every year and so the Campground is filled with Full-timers.   All you have to do is take a short walk and you can find someone to talk to. There were about 6 single ladies among the Full-timers the summer I was there. We had a bond right away. After I went to an orientation meeting for work I met a bunch of people and was invited out to eat with a group. None of us knew anything about the others. Over our meal we had a chance to get acquainted. I was the only single there but I was welcomed with open arms and minds. Everyone was fascinated by my story. I was treated like I was some sort of hero because I had picked myself up and was enjoying my Workamping experience alone. Most of the people at that first of many get togethers are still friends today.

So you see there is truly no reason to be lonely when you travel alone. Yes, you do travel alone but right outside your door is a whole world of friends just waiting to be met.

Chapter 12
Traveling

A few days before a trip I make sure my Truck and Trailer are in good working order. I always have my truck serviced prior to a long trip and check to make sure my trailer tires are properly inflated and everything is working as it should. I also carry insurance that includes road side assistance. If I have trouble on a trip all I have to do is pull to the side of the road and call for assistance.

I always figure out my route a few days before any trip. I use my road atlas as well as my computer trip software to figure out the best route for me! As I stated before I don't really like the interstates. Yes, they are good for getting from point A to point B. But you miss so much scenery that way! Besides they can be so congested. I love planning for my next trip. It can be almost as much fun as the trip itself! I look at my maps for any interesting places near my route. Usually it takes me several days before I decide just which route to take. I don't have a set in stone schedule other than the date I need to arrive at my next job. So I can take the slower route. I put my starting point and my destination in my computer. The software plots the shortest route for me then I start playing with it. I look for the secondary roads that run along the same direction. Then I look for historic sights or points of interest along the way. When I have my route planned just like I want it I save it. My GPS system will help me stay on course. It will holler Off Route, Off Route, recalculating if I deviate! The little guy that lives in my computer gets so upset if I don't stick to my plans. (Ha-ha) I have been known to tell him to hush.

One of the most difficult things for me is getting in and out of gas stations while pulling my trailer. This too has become easier with experience. You just have to learn which ones will work best. Now the very best situation is when the gas pumps are parallel to the street. When I first started out I got myself in to a tight spot I could not get out of without help. I had pulled in and filled up my tank. Then when I was ready to pull forward discovered I needed to back up to be able to swing wide enough so my trailer would not take out the gas pump. I went in the service station to ask for help and the 3 clerks behind the counter looked at me as if I had lost my mind. I told them that I just needed someone to spot for me so I did not back into anything! One of them finally consented to come out and help. Bless his heart he tried to direct me but he did not understand how backing a trailer works. I told him to just yell before I hit anything and backed up a few feet so I could get the clearance I needed not to take the pump with me! Whew....that was a close call. That station had a very narrow lot and I have learned my lesson and will not pull into one without a big drive anymore. Usually I go only about 250 miles a day and I don't have to stop to fill up. However if I spot a gas station that looks easy to maneuver I will pull over and top off my gas tank. If I stop for the night and have not filled up and have not spotted an RV friendly gas station on my way in, I will unhook my trailer and go get gas.

I do not carry much cash with me at any given time. For one thing I don't think it is safe to carry much cash. I have found it much easier to charge everything on a credit card and then pay the credit card off when the bill comes. I never carry a credit card balance over to the next month. Both of the credit cards I use pay me interest for using them. I do have an ATM card but rarely use it. My credit cards pay me a percentage to use them and my checking accounts also pay interest. So I make money by using a credit card instead of a debit card. As long as I can pay the credit card balance in full each month I make money!

This seems as good a place as any to discuss personal safety. I know a lot of people that travel with guns. I am from Texas after all. The thing about a gun is you have to be willing and able to use it! You have to ask yourself could I shoot another person. There are laws regulating guns in this country. Make sure you are following them if you decide to carry one. I do my best to give the impression that I can take care of myself. I only stop where there are a number of other people around. I am always aware of what and who is near me! I walk like I am going someplace and if someone is watching me I make a point of looking at my watch. This gives the impression I have an appointment and someone is waiting for me. I know some ladies that never lock their RV doors. I am not one of them. Mine is always locked. I can't afford to replace any of my belongings if someone should decide to take them. When I answer a knock on the door I do not open it unless I know who is outside. I rarely carry a purse. I usually carry a small wallet and my keys in my pocket. It would be a lot harder to take my wallet from my pocket than a purse off my shoulder. I take the normal precautions I would take if I lived in a regular house. I refuse to go through life scared of what might happen! There are personal safety courses available across the country. Take one; it will make you feel better about traveling alone.

If I am traveling in the off season I don't always make reservations for every night. However if I plan to spend a night in a place that I think might be busy I do call ahead. Believe me it is no fun to pull into a Campground only to find they have no room for your rig. When I was going to Iowa I had trouble finding a campground listed along the route I was taking. I had decided I would spend a night in a Wal-Mart parking lot. Some Wal-Marts allow over night parking. However just as I was ready to stop for the night I found a new campground!

Right were I needed it. To date I have not stayed over night at a Wal-Mart. Many people do. I know in my home town of Mexia Texas it is not unusual to see RVs lined up along the outside perimeter of the parking lot. This is one way to save the fee for parking in a campground over night.

Now you might be wondering how I get mail. My permanent address is my brother's home. The first year he would collect my mail for about a week then send it to me in a priority envelope. I have just this year tried the temporary forward the Post Office offers. They will forward any fist class mail for up to a year and magazines for up to two months. This works okay but it is pretty slow and I had some difficulty receiving my credit card statement in a timely manner. When you sign up for the temporary forward you give the Post Office a start and a stop date. This year I will be working in Branson Missouri for seven months. It is my plan to send in a change of address to all of the places I receive regular mail from. When I leave Branson I will change my address back to my home base address. There are companies that specialize in mail forwarding services. If you don't have someone you feel comfortable asking to take care of your mail you might consider a forwarding service. Passport America and Escapees both offer mail forwarding services. There are charges for these services but you don't run a risk of your mail getting lost. You would use the Service address as your home base and call them when you arrived at your destination to get your mail sent to you. Most are pretty flexible and will send your mail on a schedule you set. If you are traveling you can have your mail sent to you General Delivery in a town where you plan to be, even if you will only pass through. It is best to pick a small town for this! Larger towns can have more than one Post Office and you could find yourself chasing your mail around town. Be sure you call and have your mall forwarded several days before you arrive. You want the mail to be there ahead of you if you do not plan an extended stay.

As to banking I have kept the same Credit Union account that I had before I became a Workamper. I have an ATM card I can use to get cash and most of the time I get my paychecks direct deposited. If you use one of the

big chain banks such as American or Wells
Fargo you can usually find one wherever you
are across the country. I rarely use an ATM
machine to get cash. When you check out at
Wal Mart and use your debit card you can get
cash back. This saves paying the ATM fees. In
the past if my Employer did not use direct
deposit I would mail my deposit to my bank.
You do run the risk of it getting lost in the mail
if you choose to do this. Otherwise you can also
open an account at a local bank and then close it
when you move again.

Chapter 13
Can you afford the RV Lifestyle?

I guess the next important question to be answered is: Can I afford the full-time RV lifestyle? The short answer is yes, if you don't have a huge debt hanging over your head.

When I first started out I had half of the debt we had accumulated while married, but I also owned half of the home we had to sell. My pickup was paid off a couple of months before I took my first workamper job. So at least I did not have that to worry about. While I was out in Big Bend I had the closing papers on our home mailed to me and I signed them out there. I arranged for my brother to go and pick up my check and deposit it into my bank account. I was then able to sit down and pay off every bill I owed. Talk about a good feeling! I even had some left over to put away for a rainy day. It does make a big difference if you can go into full-timing with a clean slate as far as debt is concerned. I have friends that have a tough time because they have debt. Most Workamping jobs are not high paying jobs. My jobs have paid between $6.25 and $11.50 an hour. However, some of them have also included an RV site. At most of my jobs I have worked between 30 and 40 hours a week. There are some campgrounds that hire people to work for site only but I have not done that yet. If you have retirement income you may not have to work many hours to make ends meet.

You also have to keep in mind that there will be times when you are between jobs. One of the great things about being a Workamper is being able to decide when and where you want to work. It is also much harder to find that winter job. Face it most of us don't want to live in the North during the cold months. So there is more competition for the limited number of winter jobs in the south. It is however, easy to find a holiday position at a retail establishment.

There are on going bills we all have each month. Make a list of yours and figure out what it will take for you to be able to make it. For me, I have a cell phone, Dish network, auto insurance and a truck payment (I traded in my 1999 for a 2005 last year). There are also those yearly expenses like my RV insurance. Figure up how much you spend on groceries, clothes, and entertainment each month. Now gasoline can be a big variable as we all know. You will just have to give this your best guess. Most of the time when I am working, I either live on site, or very near my work. The farthest I have been from work is 4 ½ miles. Living near work cuts way down on my gasoline expense! Only two months of last year was I too far away to walk to work. I worked eight months out of the year. I will not get rich Workamping. While my income is not all that great, I find that I live a very comfortable life. My bills are relatively small so in comparison my income does not have to be big. Last year I had one job that included my site, one job where the campsite fee was deducted from my salary and one where I paid the site fee. The lowest fee was of course $0 and the highest I paid was $395 a month. By the way the value of your site is considered taxable income unless required to live there by your employer. I personally prefer to have my site fee taken out of my pay check! My monthly ongoing bills total only about $300 a month including my truck payment (my trade was free of debt and I made a large down payment). I am hoping to have it paid off by this time next year.

I usually don't spend all I have coming in when I am working, so it leaves me a reserve for that yearly insurance and taking time off between jobs. My expenses do fluctuate depending on how much traveling I do. It is much less expensive to spend a month in one place than to pay a nightly fee. I have found campgrounds where you can stay for as little as $200 a month plus electricity. Right now I am parked in my brother's driveway and I pay him $100 a month to cover any extra utilities he incurs because I am here. He does not ask that I pay this; it just makes me feel better. I must admit now that this is not my only income. I receive ½ of my ex-husband's retirement each month. While it is not enough to live on, it does give me a cushion to fall back on if needed. It allowed me to go into debt for that new truck without worrying about whether I could afford the debt. If you need more income you can spend less time off than I do and go straight from one Workamping job to the next with little break between. Only you know what your needs are. It is also possible to work a full time "regular" job and live in an RV. I have known several people that have done this until they could get all their bills paid off.

The best way to figure out if you can afford to live full time in an RV is figure out what your monthly bills are. If you are in debt it is much harder to make ends meet! Get out the calculator and total up your on going expenses. On average last year I made $1,375 each month from Workamper jobs. Can you live on this? What about the down times when you are not working? The big thing is not to depend on a certain amount each month. As I said my income and expenses fluctuate. I try to keep my monthly expenses in the range of $1,000 or less. This allows me to build up a reserve for the times when I am not working. I don't spend more than I can afford to pay in any given month. Never carry over credit card debit! If you have trouble with charging and paying off your credit card every month use a Debit card instead. I can cut expenses by eating at home instead of going out. I can also greatly cut my gas expenses by traveling less. Walking to work is great exercise and it is free!

This is the walking path to my work in Yellowstone.

I also bought a small electric scooter to
ride to work when I was at Adventureland.
There are a lot of entertaining things to do that
are free! I do a lot of getting out in nature and
walking. I have visited covered bridges, sat
around a campfire and had pot lucks with
friends. All of these things can be more fun than
going out to eat at an expensive restaurant. It is
possible to have a great life full timing and not
need a huge income.

Chapter 14
The Full-time Workamping lifestyle

I was asked the other day if I was moving up the job ladder? Give me a break! There are no ladders to climb. If I wanted a career and to climb ladders I would be working in the cooperate world. The lady that asked me the question looked at me as if I had lost my mind when I told her there was not a ladder to climb, in my line of work! Part of the enjoyment of Workamping is I have no stress! Yes, sometimes the jobs are demanding and physical but the worries are someone else's! In all of my Workamping jobs I have had to deal with the public. I have found for the most part people on vacation are happy. You can always tell the ones that just arrived! They are usually still stressed and in a hurry. I have worked with a few workampers that try to run things. These folks always think they know better than the management. They are frequently the most, unhappy and complaining people to deal with. Yes, occasionally I will make a suggestion to management. I leave it there. If they decide to follow my suggestion, great, if not that is okay too. I am just there to do the best job I can and draw my paycheck so I can keep on going.

For me part of the joy of Workamping is being able to take a month or so off at a time, to just enjoy living! I also love the challenges of each new job. A lot of workampers get stuck in a rut and return each year to the same jobs. I am determined that at least once every year I will go someplace different. I can't tell you how much fun it is to live in a new area long enough to absorb some of the local traditions and get to know the area. I was amazed at how much there was to see and do in Iowa. Iowa was never on the top of any vacation list I ever made. I guess you have figured out by now that Yes, I got the job at Adventureland Amusement Park my first summer Workamping. I worked games as an attendant at the park. While it was not a mentally challenging job it was difficult to stand in one spot for hours! The good thing was, there were about twelve to fourteen different game booths each in three different areas of the park, and we rotated. So I usually did not work the same game two days in a row. While at times it could be boring, at other times I was so busy I hardly had time to think. Usually the morning hours are pretty dull in the games areas, because when people rush in the gates, they head straight for the rides. I highly recommend working at Adventureland. The folks that own the park are super people to work for. They have been hiring workampers for so many years that their program is one of the best I have seen. They even have an employee canteen where we took our breaks, and would eat an inexpensive meal, on the days we worked. One thing to be aware of, if you decide to work at Adventureland, is that it gets HOT and humid in Iowa in the late summer. You will be working outside so be prepared to be warm. If you don't like amusement parks don't go there. I went with an open mind and loved it.

Me working at Adventureland

I plan to one day return to work another season at Adventureland. I made so many friends there, and we had a great time together. When the park first opens in the spring, it is only open weekends, so you work two days and are off five. This gives you plenty of time to get acquainted with your fellow workampers, and to do some sight seeing in the area. That spring I went to the Pella Tulip festival, visited John Wayne's birth place, and the covered bridges of Madison County, with some of my new found friends. It even snowed a little the first weekend the park was open! Adventureland is located on the North East side of Des Moines in the suburb of Altoona. I loved the small town atmosphere of the area. I am a country girl at heart and big cities hold no attraction for me. I only went into Des Moines itself a few times. Altoona had everything I needed. We started having pool parties every Tuesday night at the campground pool. They would close the pool at 9 o'clock to everyone but workampers. We had some grand times sitting next to the pool eating snacks and discussing our days working. Some of us would occasionally even take a dip in the pool. During June, July and August we were all working so hard that we did not do a lot of visiting or sightseeing beyond the regular weekly pool parties. However in August Iowa has its State Fair. This is a must see for anyone in the area. I had never seen a butter cow before! They had a display of a life-size cow sculpted out of butter! It was so realistic.

Butter Cow at Iowa State Fair

    You can also get most anything to eat on a stick. The most popular being a pork chop! They had designated areas scattered around Des Moines where you could park and hop a bus to get to the fair. This is wonderful because parking is limited near the fairgrounds.

    In September the park is only open on weekends so we spent our extra time off really exploring. There were trips planned to just about every tourist attraction in the area. Adventureland sponsored a trip to the Des Moines Zoo and to the Mall of America. A group of us also floated down the Iowa River on inner tubes visited the Amana colonies, and Road the Scenic Boone Valley Railroad. We also had pot luck suppers at least once a week. There were usually more things planned to do than I had the energy to do. We generally enjoyed ourselves to the max!

Workamping in the Big Bend area and in Yellowstone were both amazing experiences. I love nature and both of these National parks certainly abound with nature. They were totally different experiences. Big Bend while somewhat mountainous is also very arid and dry. I had not spent any time in a desert area before and really enjoyed exploring. I was surprised that water could be found in places where I never expected to see it. The part of Texas where I grew up is nothing like The Big Bend area of the state. Most of it looks like a scene out of an old west movie. And some of the characters that live there look like they stepped right out of a movie. I spent February and March there my first year Workamping. I went back for the same time period last year, as I felt there were things I had missed seeing the first time. The second time I went out there I was able to take more of the hiking trails with fellow workampers. We had the same days off once a week and were able to explore the park. It truly is an amazing place to see. Just driving the roads you see some awesome views. When you get off the main roads and hike some of the trails you get even more of an up close and personal feel for the place. It is one of those places that just feel old! The winter or Spring is the best time to visit Big Bend. The desert came alive in the spring! I did not expect to see so many things blooming.

Yucca blooming in Big Bend National Park

Yellowstone has always been special to me. I remember the first vacation my family ever took to Yellowstone. It will be a trip I remember the rest of my life with fondness. This past summer I spent working there was truly a unique experience. I have never lived where I had to look outside before I stepped out. If you RV in Yellowstone you always need to be aware that not all your neighbors are people. While I never had a bear at my door, there were several occasions when there were Elk in my yard. I even had one peeking in my window once!

Elk behind my trailer

I worked with a number of foreign college students while at Yellowstone. There were also a lot of older employees. Yellowstone General Stores does a good job of hiring a real diverse group of employees. The students and some older folks live in dorms while at Yellowstone. The students usually do not have transportation. On my days off when I planned an outing, I would let the students know, so any could tag along that wanted too. There was one evening when I decided to go up to the Grand Canyon of the Yellowstone. I had three languages being spoken in my truck! Besides all of the wonders of living in Yellowstone for a whole summer, the opportunity to get to know young people from other parts of the world was great.

There are so many things to do in and around Yellowstone that I will have to go back one of these years!

When I left Yellowstone it took me a couple of weeks to get back to Texas. I did not have to report to my next job until November, and it was the end of September. So I took the opportunity and enjoyed my trip. I spent a couple of nights in Riverton Wyoming at the Windriver RV Park. I had only planned on staying one night but it was so pleasant there I stayed two nights. Then I traveled on to Ft. Laramie Wyoming. I had planned to just travel through, but when I discovered the Fort decided to spend an extra day. While in the area I stayed at the Pony Soldier RV Park.

Barracks at Ft. Laramie

The reason I had taken that route was I wanted to see Scottsbluff in Nebraska. So Ft. Laramie was a bonus. When you travel try to allow enough time to do some sightseeing. I never know what I might find around the next corner or over the next hill. I have learned to enjoy my travels, and no longer just hurry down the road to get to my next stop. I highly recommend slowing down and enjoying the sights.

I have told you about just a few of my experiences. Maybe one of these days we will meet beside a campfire and I can tell you more! Trust me, if I can do this anyone can! You just have to believe you can! If I had not tried full timing it would have stayed a dream. I have not regretted my decision to hit the road. Years from now I will not be looking back and say I wish I had! I did it! Yes, you can too!

When Workampers part; we rarely say good-bye. So instead of the end I think I will just say: I hope to, See You down the road!

On the road and loving it!

Favorite Websites

I thought that I would conclude with a list of my favorite websites. Some of them having nothing to do with RVing.....I just like them. They are listed in alphabetical order.

Amazon   www.amazon.com
Americas Best Campground   www.abc-branson.com
Blockbuster   www.blockbuster.com
Branson.com   www.branson.com
Cool Works   www.coolworks.com
First RV   www.firstrv.com
Foremost Insurance
www.foremostinsurance.com
Fort Worth RV Show
www.fortworthrvshow.com
Full Time RVer   www.fulltimerver.com
Gamesville   www.gamesville.com
Good Sam Club   www.goodsamclub.com
Google   www.google.com
I Won   www.iwon.com
Jackies Creations   www.crafty-ones.com/web/viewbooth.asp?boothID=539
KOA   www.koa.com

Lulu	www.lulu.com
My RV Space	www.myrvspace.com
Netflix	www.netflix.com
Old Faithful	

www.nps.gov/archive/yell/oldfaithfulcam.htm

National Park Service	www.nps.gov
NPS temporary jobs	www.sep.nps.gov
Passport America	

www.passportamerica.com

Pioneer River Resort

www.pioneerriverresort.com

RV America	www.rvamerica.com
RV Bookstore	http://rvbookstore.com
RV Travel	www.rvtravel.com
RV USA	www.rvusa.com
See's Candies	www.seescandies.com
Snag A Job	www.snagajob.com
Texas Parks and Wildlife	www.tpwd.state.tx.us
Woodalls	www.woodalls.com
Workamper News	www.workamper.com
Workers on Wheels	

www.workersonwheels.com

Yahoo	www.yahoo.com

CPSIA information can be obtained at www.ICGtesting.com
Printed in the USA
LVOW12s0819060314

376282LV00002B/519/P